MEXICO

Tracy Vonder Brink

TABLE OF CONTENTS

A Crabtree Seedlings Book

School-to-Home Support for Caregivers and Teachers

This book helps children grow by letting them practice reading. Here are a few guiding questions to help the reader with building his or her comprehension skills. Possible answers appear here in red.

Before Reading:

- What do I think this book is about?
    - *I think this book is about Mexico.*
    - *I think this book is about places to visit in Mexico.*
- What do I want to learn about this topic?
    - *I want to learn where Mexico is.*
    - *I want to learn about the kinds of animals that live in Mexico.*

During Reading:

- I wonder why...
    - *I wonder why monarch butterflies fly to Mexico in winter.*
    - *I wonder why there are so many volcanoes in Mexico.*
- What have I learned so far?
    - *I have learned that Mexico is in North America.*
    - *I have learned that the Chihuahuan Desert is the largest desert in North America.*

After Reading:

- What details did I learn about this topic?
    - *I have learned that Mexico City is Mexico's biggest city.*
    - *I have learned that Mexico has rain forests.*
- Read the book again and look for the vocabulary words.
    - *I see the word* ***desert*** *on page 10, and the word* ***ruins*** *on page 20. The other glossary words are on pages 22 and 23.*

Mexico is a country.

It is in **North America**.

Mexico City is the **capital**.

It is Mexico's biggest city.

Most people in Mexico speak Spanish.

More than 22 million people live in Mexico City.

Mexico City has many beautiful churches.

The Metropolitan Cathedral sits in the city's center.

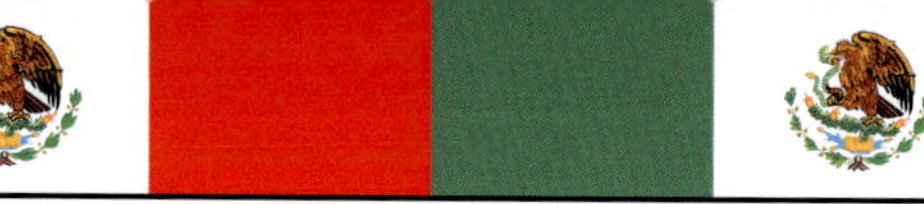

Mexico has more than 3,000 volcanoes.

Popocatépetl is near Mexico City.

This volcano puts out steam or ash almost every day.

The Chihuahuan **Desert** stretches across the North.

It is the largest desert in North America.

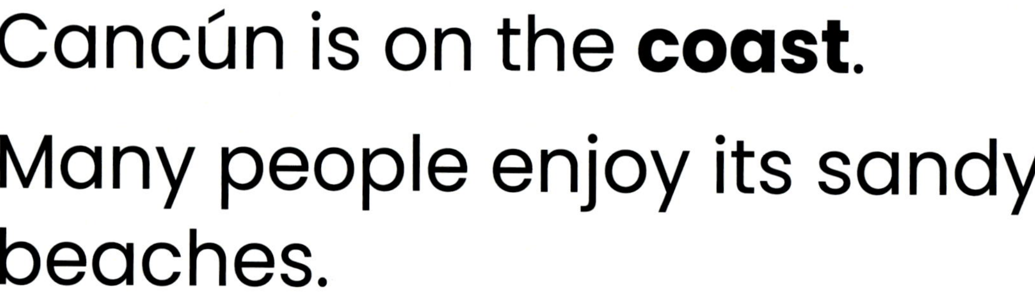

Cancún is on the **coast**.

Many people enjoy its sandy beaches.

The Sierra Madre mountain range is in Mexico.

Every year, monarch butterflies fly from the U.S. and Canada to spend the winter there.

Rain forests are found in southern Mexico.

Thousands of kinds of plants and animals live there.

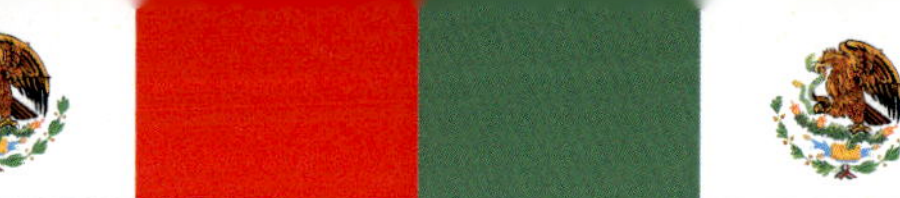

Mexican spider monkeys swing through the rain forest.

Margays hunt and sleep in the treetops.

A margay is a small, wild cat. It can run up and down trees.

Chichén Itzá is an **ancient** city in Yucatán state.

Its **ruins** are more than 1,000 years old.

Mexico is an exciting place!

Glossary

ancient (EYN-chent): Belonging to a time that was long ago

capital (KAP-i-tl): The city where the government of a country or a state is located

coast (kohst): The land next to the ocean or sea

desert (DEH-zert): A very hot, dry area that gets a small amount of rain per year

North America (NORTH uh-MEH-rih-kuh): One of Earth's seven continents

rain forest (RAYN faw-ruhst): A dense, tropical forest that has a large amount of rainfall

ruins (ROO-unz): A city or buildings that have been destroyed

Index

About the Author

Tracy Vonder Brink

Tracy Vonder Brink loves to visit new places. She has visited Mexico and enjoyed seeing Mexico City. She lives in Cincinnati, Ohio, with her husband, two daughters, and two rescue dogs.

Written by: Tracy Vonder Brink
Designed by: Rhea Magaro
Series Development: James Earley
Proofreader: Melissa Boyce
Educational Consultant: Marie Lemke M.Ed.

Photographs: All images from Shutterstock

Crabtree Publishing

crabtreebooks.com 800-387-7650

Printed in the U.S.A./062024/CG20240201

Published in Canada
Crabtree Publishing
616 Welland Avenue
St. Catharines, Ontario
L2M 5V6

Published in the United States
Crabtree Publishing
347 Fifth Avenue
Suite 1402-145
New York, New York, 10016

Library and Archives Canada Cataloguing in Publication
Available at Library and Archives Canada

Library of Congress Cataloging-in-Publication Data
Available at the Library of Congress

Hardcover: 978-1-0398-4476-6
Paperback: 978-1-0398-4557-2
Ebook (pdf): 978-1-0398-4629-6
Epub: 978-1-0398-4699-9
Read-Along: 978-1-0398-4769-9
Audio: 978-1-0398-4839-9